ALSO BY CALVIN TRILLIN

Deciding the Next Decider

CALVIN TRILLIN

Deciding the Next Decider

The 2008 Presidential Race in Rhyme

RANDOM HOUSE   NEW YORK

Published in the United States by Random House, an imprint of
The Random House Publishing Group, a division of
Random House, Inc., New York.

RANDOM HOUSE and colophon are registered trademarks
of Random House, Inc.

The narrative poem that constitutes the bulk of this book
appears here for the first time. Some of
the poems embedded in it originally appeared
in *The Nation*.

Library of Congress Cataloging-in-Publication Data

Trillin, Calvin.
Deciding the next decider : the 2008 presidential race in rhyme/ Calvin Trillin.
p.   cm.
ISBN 978-1-4000-6828-9
1. Presidents—United States—Election—2008—Poetry.
2. Presidential candidates—United States—Poetry. I. Title.
PS3570.R5D43 2008
811'.54—dc22   2008040410

Printed in the United States of America on acid-free paper

www.atrandom.com

246897531

FIRST EDITION

Book design by Carole Lowenstein

To Alex and Brian—two daddy laureates.

Contents

Deciding the Next Decider

1

Let the Games Begin

Whatever problems Washington is facing,
Campaigning is what gets its blood a-racing.
Before the '06 midterm vote was in,
The top consultants there began to spin
Scenarios about that vote and why
It showed '08 was natural for their guy.
But as the midterm voting day drew near,
The GOP began to have some fear
That they'd be beaten right across the nation.
Here's how the press surmised the situation:
The Bush economy is out to sea,
And scandals now have rocked the GOP.
Its leadership had known for quite a while
They harbored there on their side of the aisle
A person who for absolutely ages
Was sending come-on notes to teenage pages.

And Bush's war, still raging unsubsided?
It's clear by now that voters have decided
His war's a crime—and as the leading perp he's
About as high up in the polls as herpes.

We Got Those Wall-to-Wall 24/7 Damage-Control Blues

(As sung by the Bush Administration's Down Home Singers)

They leaked that NIE that said Iraq's
Producing terrorists and such in stacks,
So even winning sort of means to lose.
We got those wall-to-wall 24/7 damage-control blues.

Then Woodward writes that Bush is bubble boy—
As clueless as those dudes defending Troy—
And Rumsfeld is a Queeg with shortened fuse.
We got those wall-to-wall 24/7 damage-control blues.

Then Foley's creepy messages appear,
And Dennis Hastert's known for a year,
So he can't claim the leaders had no clues.
Iraq each day brings worse, more violent news.
If we can't find some gays to bash, we'll lose.
This stuff could drive the boss man back to booze.
We got those wall-to-wall 24/7 damage-control blues.

The GOP felt land about to slide—
An attitude Karl Rove could not abide.
Republicans will triumph, Rove insisted.
Had he hatched plots, nefarious and twisted?

One Possible Explanation for Karl Rove's Confidence About the Midterm Elections

One simple stroke by Rove could yet erase
The burdens that the GOP has carried:
They'd simply say they'd foiled a bombing plot
By two gay Muslims who had just been married.

But Rove was wrong. The midterm was a rout.
Whatever that election was about,
Whichever words Bush used as a disclaimer,
This lame duck president was now much lamer.
He said he'd work with Democrats once more.
That's sort of what he'd said six years before—
Before, that is, he saw himself as Thor
Destroying evil in a holy war.
He tried to reestablish some rapport
By showing Donald Rumsfeld out the door.

An Opponent of the War Attempts to Say Farewell to Donald Rumsfeld with at Least a Modicum of Courtesy

The killing in Iraq's gone on this long
Because you think the strong can't say they're wrong.
To be so wrong so often is a curse,
But being arrogantly wrong is worse.
Still, briefings were a hoot. Our favorite feature?
That tone—exactly like a third-grade teacher
Explaining math to those forevermore
Too slow to get promoted to grade four.
So may you find, as down life's road you're wending,
More folks to whom you're always condescending.

Though many found Don Rumsfeld's exit pleasing,
Approval ratings stayed well south of freezing.
So Bush was done, observers would contend:
His term had ended long before the end.
Within just weeks, the presidential story
Was whose committees were exploratory.
And bloggers speculated who might join
Newt Gingrich, spotted lurking in Des Moines,
Where Edwards had so often paid a call
He'd almost lost his Carolina drawl.

And others were beginning to remember
The beauty of a cornfield in December.

After Tuning in to the Sunday Talk Shows to See What the Sabbath Gasbags Have to Say

They talk of nothing but '08
And who'll emerge triumphant when
The voting booths are finally closed.
But what are we to do 'til then?

The Democrats said what we need is change
From Bush. Well, sure, but here is something strange:
Republicans themselves could not ignore
Katrina and the wretched, endless war.
A lot of them—with some regrets, it's true—
Now seemed inclined to run against him too.

2

The Almost-Rans: Republicans

Republican insiders once agreed,
When contemplating who'd most likely lead
Their presidential ticket in '08,
George Allen was the perfect candidate.
He fit what's often valued by the Right:
Quite cheerful, Reaganesque, and not too bright.
His '06 Senate race was called a breeze,
But then one comment brought him to his knees.
He said "macaca" in a way that fully
Revealed that he was nothing but a bully.
The deed was done that fast: Within a beat
This man was set to lose his Senate seat.
One message should have then been learned by all:
That YouTube's always lurking in the hall.

YouTube

(*Sung to the tune of "Hambone"*)

YouTube, YouTube,
What you got?
Allen in a nasty spot.
With that spot his bid goes south.
Allen should have watched his mouth.
Allen's race is over; it's
Victim of a million hits.
YouTube!

For just a while it seemed that George Pataki,
A long shot, might attempt to pull a Rocky
(Balboa, never Rockefeller—no,
The Right holds him a traitor to his dough).
Pataki said he wasn't in the game,
And Gilmore of Virginia said the same.
Another early favorite, Doctor Frist,
The senator, was stricken from the list.
Though as a Senate leader, Bill Frist had
What might have been a mighty launching pad,
Some problems came along, the worst one being
A blind trust that seemed capable of seeing.
Around then Gingrich said, to be quite frank, he
Himself was guilty of some hanky-panky

While he, with brazen sanctimony preached
That sinful Clinton had to be impeached.
Observers seemed to think what Newt had done
Was clear the air so he could later run.
But Newt, unlikely Hamlet, changed his mind
A couple times at least, and then declined.

3

The Almost-Rans: Democrats

And who in Clinton's party would compete
With Hillary, the candidate to beat?
The big mules of the party'd coalesced
Around her. Fat cats lined up to invest.
Republicans were loading their artillery,
Assuming they'd be aiming it at Hillary.
Although hardworking, smart, plugged in, incisive,
She was, some said, alarmingly divisive.
And would the voters vote for in the fall
A woman for the biggest job of all?
She was ahead, but suffered from this spin:
She'd get the nomination, then not win.
So some, although they didn't use this trope,
Had started searching for the Great Male Hope.
Some thought that Wesley Clark and Evan Bayh
Were sounding like they might just make a try.

Mark Warner of Virginia had panache.
He had the looks. He also had the cash.
But Clark and Bayh declined to go ahead,
And Warner sought a Senate seat instead.
And in the background always was Al Gore,
Who, after all, may well have won before.
(In *Bush v. Gore,* the court of strict construction
Had, thanks to some miraculous deduction,
Decided that the Framers, in this case,
Would want no voting recount to take place.)
Gore's film on warming and our pending doom
Might launch, some thought, a presidential boom.
Some said that if the presidential glimmer
Was in Gore's eyes he'd try to get much slimmer:
Presumably, they looked for photo ops
To see what Gore was stuffing in his chops,
And also if, as far as they could judge, he
Was looking rather trim or rather pudgy.

A Political Reporter Laments Being Assigned to Watch Al Gore's Waistline

This job means sometimes digging up the dirt
On if a pol has stolen or he's cheating
With some cute waitress from a D.C. bar.
But who knew I'd be tracking what he's eating?

My editor, the clever dog, decided
The way to check that presidential itch is
To follow Gore, especially at meals,
And see if he stays too big for his britches.

Last week, I told my desk that Gore might run,
Though he appeared to be at least full-size:
A waiter at a Georgetown place revealed
Gore's order had included "hold the fries."

But now a source will swear that he was there
When Gore demolished half a cow, then stowed
Away in sixty seconds gobs of pie.
Two pieces. Apple crumble. A la mode.

My major back in school was poli-sci—
Quite valuable, I thought, for this position.
I know now, though, for covering Al Gore,
I should have studied diet and nutrition.

Tom Vilsack joined the race for just a minute.
He quit before folks knew that he was in it.
Russ Feingold, early, bid the fray good-bye.
Al Sharpton had some other fish to fry.
Did all that sure-thing talk of Clinton mean
She'd be the one contender on the scene?
No, some pols sought to beat this tough mam'selle—
Some seven, if you're counting Mike Gravel.

4

Obama, Rising

Electrified is what they were, they say—
The Democrats in Boston on the day
A man with eloquence at his command
Had held the whole convention in his hand.
Their highest campaign moment in '04
Was when Barack Obama had the floor.
He spoke of getting past our old divides—
To form one nation, not just many sides.
He said together we'd heal every wound.
The crowd exploded. Why, they nearly swooned.
He hadn't made it to the Senate yet,
But, still, some delegates were moved to bet
That he was destined for the next top spot.
They made such statements, Hillary or not.
When Kerry lost, the buzz did not abate.
Some said Barack could well afford to wait.

He had, they said, no end of times to run:
In twenty twelve he'd be but fifty-one.
According to a long-established tenet,
He should mature for years yet in the Senate.
(Producing legislation at a trickle,
Some Senate members don't mature, they pickle.)
Obama, thinking time would not improve
The chance he had, resolved to make his move.
He went to Springfield, where he could invoke
The spirit of Abe Lincoln as he spoke
To thousands, cheering in the bitter cold.
He may have been by many fans extolled,
But pros said it was still a long-shot bet
To think the nomination's what he'd get.
When faced with Clinton's powerful machine,
They said, he might collapse, like Howard Dean.
Experience was what he seemed to lack.
And to be frank, they pointed out, he's black.

5

←——→

Pacifying Preachers

The nominee is easy to discern
Among Republicans: They go in turn.
(Republicans think order is sublime.
They dress in suits. Their meetings start on time.)
Among these red-state types it wouldn't do
To have some guy appear out of the blue.
They even balked when Reagan first ignored
The rules and tried to push ahead of Ford.
Bush One came after Ron, as was expected.
Bob Dole, whose turn it was, then got selected.
(The wait was years and years and years for Dole—
Until he was the age of Old King Cole.)
And then Bush Two—much firmer than his pop.
The flip-flop's not for him; no, just the flop.

The Great Decider

(A short adaptation of the Buck Ram song for the Platters, sung by George W. Bush)

Oh yes I'm the great decider (ooh ooh).
I'm resolute, and I am strong (ooh ooh).
I've said a prayer, so no need to care
If all my decisions are wrong.

So John McCain now seemed to be at bat.
The Christian Right was less than pleased by that.
He's pro-life, but they tended to believe
He failed to wear his Jesus on his sleeve.
Before, when his cup ranneth to the brim,
They'd slandered both his family and him.
McCain, who'd finished number two to Two,
Believed his turn was now long overdue.
As he assumed the role of Bush Two's heir,
A somewhat different John McCain was there.
No longer did he seem the same man who
Had charmed the voters (and reporters, too)
With candor as he'd cheerfully express
His willingness to call BS BS.
Eight years before, by nature or design,
He seemed compelled to cross his party's line.
He still did cross, but only now and then,

And much more cautiously than way back when.
The preachers he once treated with disdain
Were paid obeisance by this John McCain.
Still, pollsters and the pundits all agreed
That John McCain did not start in the lead.
No, in the lead was one come-lately-Johnny:
A pro-choice mayor named Rudy Giuliani.
Alone, at least according to his version,
He'd saved New York from total crime immersion,
And, after 9/11's horrors there,
Was thought of as America's main mayor.
(Though people in New York who really knew him
Replied America was welcome to him.)

An Out-of-Towner Questions a New Yorker About America's Mayor

*"So tell me the most charming feature then
Of he who saved the city from collapse."
"It might take me a while to think of that.
Offhand, I'd say vindictiveness, perhaps."*

The third contender in the leading three,
Mitt Romney, guaranteed the Right that he
Opposed abortion, though he had already
Defended it when he got beat by Teddy.

By then the preachers of the Christian Right
Were saying true believers had a plight:
The candidates who firmly held their views
Were those most politicians thought would lose.
Mike Huckabee was fundless and obscure,
And Brownback seemed unlikely to endure.
The likely winners all seemed slightly pagan,
And none of them resembled Ronald Reagan.
But those whose social views had been abhorred
Assured the preachers they were now on board.
Since Bush the First, those running in this race
Knew well that they must mollify the Base.
Yes, mollify, although that might invite
The phrase "a lapdog of the Christian Right."

Some Former Backsliders Try to Please the Christian Right

Although he mortified himself, it's true,
By showing up at Jerry Falwell U,
And says that every effort should be made
To guarantee reversing Roe v. Wade,
The Christian Right's big mullahs make it plain
They're still not comfortable with John McCain.

And Giuliani's heel is like Achilles':
Revolving fillies give the Right the willies.
His other heel is pretty much the same,

Since bashing gays was never Rudy's game.
He says that he himself, right from the start,
Despised abortion deeply in his heart.

Mitt Romney's saying now he should have known
A stem cell's just a human, not quite grown.
Gay marriage, which he used to think was good,
Is now the sort of awful thing that should
Be banned by an amendment he would urge
To rid us finally of this evil scourge.

A shelter full of lapdogs with one plea:
"Oh, take me home! Oh, please! Oh, please pick me!"

One candidate the Right still hoped to see
Was big Fred Thompson, since they knew that he
Would always, as he'd done on *Law & Order,*
Protect the unborn and our southern border.
He had the common touch, they said, and more.
But Thompson just continued to explore.
He'd figured, maybe, he'd be really dumb
To hurry into that unseemly scrum.
While fans became increasingly fanatic,
Fred waited for the moment most dramatic.
He had an actor's skills at his command;
They all know that one's entrance must be grand—
Upstage, of course, as if you own that zone,
And, most importantly of all, alone.

6

Independentistas

This Michael Bloomberg is a small, rich smartie
Who isn't comfortable in either party.
From Democrat, in New York's fateful fall,
He switched so he could run for City Hall.
Six years from then, he left the GOP,
Reviving talk among the pols that he
Might try an independent White House go—
Self-financed, in the style of Ross Perot.
Comparing them, Mike's Carville, Kevin Sheekey,
Saw Mike as just as rich and much less squeaky.
A moderate who's rarely overwrought,
Mike seemed nonpartisan, and it was thought
If parties chose extremes, then he could enter
And run successfully right down the center.
His drawbacks? Well, his speeches, some would gripe,
Can mimic Ambien, the CR type.

Perot made Bloomberg somewhat déjà vu–ish.
And to be frank, they pointed out, he's Jewish.
Despite the speculation, Mike explained
That mayoral duties in New York remained.
He said he planned to stay there at his desk,
But that was not considered Shermanesque.
That sort of "no" was simply being cunning;
So rumor had it Mike was in the running.

What Could You Buy for What It Costs to Run for President?

You surely could tell your accountant or lawyer
To buy you a boat, say a largeish destroyer.
Or maybe a house is much more what you'd dig—
Like Buckingham Palace, except twice as big.
For that kind of money, it's cool to have both.
But still that's no match for your taking that oath
Of office that leaves you with one sure belief:
Wherever you go, they'll play "Hail to the Chief."

His close friends said that Mike would not jump in
Unless he had a fighting chance to win.
Of Nader, this, of course, would not be true.
Just why Ralph runs is harder to construe.
He claims the major parties are the same.

So it's okay to play the spoiler's game.
(With facts this view is in direct collision.
For instance, in the Civil Rights division,
Which civil rights are Justice lawyers liable
To push—the right to vote or teach the Bible?)
Most people think that Ralph did what he did
Eight years before from ego, maybe id.
So no one was surprised when Nader said
In '08 that he planned to go ahead
And run. The Democrats did not act scared.
In fact, it seemed not many people cared.

As Daffodils Come Out in the Spring

So Nader's going to run again.
The Times *put that on page fifteen.*
There's nothing that's much sadder than
An ego trip that's barely seen.

Republicans had also seen a sign
Of some third-party static down the line.
Ron Paul, a libertarian and doc,
Had fans like those enjoyed by kings of rock.
Quite antiwar and antitax, Ron Paul
Just didn't want much government at all.

Just Leave Us Be

(*A Libertarian request to government, sung by Ron Paul to the tune of Irving Berlin's "What'll I Do?"*)

Just leave us be.
Your regs are agony.
This is our plea:
Just leave us be.

Just leave us be.
Please shrink in vast degree.
Leave markets free.
Just leave us be.

Just leave us be, and leave the IRS
To atrophy—no Schedule C.

Just leave us be.
With fewer laws you'll see
Real liberty.
Just leave us be.

Republicans feared Paul's fans wouldn't scatter
But find a candidate who just might matter.
Long after Michael Bloomberg's bid was done,

Another candidate announced he'd run:
Bob Barr, of Georgia, came from quite a thicket
Of Libertarians to lead their ticket.
So Barr became the Nader of the Right—
No less self-righteous and no more contrite.

7

Iowa on Their Mind

Some worthies from the Senate threw their hats
Into the presidential ring, and that's
Routine, except a lot of hats were floating
A year or so before the Iowa voting.
To Iowa the candidates would make
A trip if there were fourteen hands to shake.
They covered all the state like morning dew,
All aching just to have a word with you.
For months on end, you'd find yourself hard put
To find a place where they weren't underfoot.
In diners, you'd begin to find it odd
If you weren't joined by Biden or Chris Dodd.
You try to do some shopping at the mall,
But at the mall you can't escape Ron Paul.
You're all alone, it's dark, a man's pursuing.
He says, "I'm Duncan Hunter. How you doing?"

You think, relieved, he's some new friendly resident,
But, no, this man is running hard for president.
At church, you hear, as you're about to pray,
"My name's John Edwards. How are you today?"
And you say, "Nice to see you, my name's Luke.
Last week, I met you three times in Dubuque."

Yes, I Know He's a Mill Worker's Son but There's Hollywood in That Hair
(*A country song about John Edwards*)

He grew up poor in Carolina, sure.
He's not a fake. He comes from folks like us.
I like the sound of what John Edwards says,
But why's his hair the kind that plain won't muss?
Yes, I know he's a mill worker's son, but there's Hollywood
  in that hair.

He whacks the corporations where it hurts.
His plan is best for caring for the sick.
His wife's a gem. We're nuts about the kids.
But Lordy that man's pompadour's too slick.
Yes, I know he's a mill worker's son, but there's Hollywood
  in that hair.
Sure I know he's got substance and grit, and judging by
  hair is not fair.

> *Yes, I know he's a genuine guy, and there's plain people's*
> *values we share.*
> *Yes, I know he's a mill worker's son, but there's Hollywood*
> *in that hair.*

Until attracting Jimmy Carter's eye,
These caucuses were minor, and here's why:
All candidates who've seriously contended
Agree the rules cannot be comprehended.
And who's ahead is always hard to say:
Who knows who'll go to caucus and who'll stay
Through boring speeches and the odd dispute
About rules well designed to convolute?
And who knows if the straw vote at the fair
Reflects support that's really truly there
Or very simply in its ledger logs
Those visitors less interested in hogs.
This bugs reporters, too, because they treasure
A horse race they can quantify and measure.
And even nationwide that sort of toting
Was hard, since there'd be months before the voting.
So, looking for some metric they could count,
They settled easily on the amount
Of money candidates had taken in,
And thus declared that Romney might well win.

On the News That Mitt Romney Finished First Among Republicans in First-Quarter Fund-Raising

To play the role of president Mitt fit:
His jaw is square. No wives have ever split.
His mug's unblemished by the smallest zit.
On looks alone a jury would acquit.
But Mitt's campaign was not seen as a hit.
On every poll he lagged by quite a bit.
Then donor forms all candidates submit
Revealed a bunch of money went to Mitt.
(Which means each donor holds from Mitt a chit.)
So Mitt as candidate is now legit.
The pundits now aren't writing Mitt's obit.
If one thing counts, they think, then money's it.

8

Show Me the Money

So funds were needed. Campaign costs were mounting.
And who snared funds became a way of counting—
A way to say, with voting months away,
Which candidates might leave and which might stay.
With Internet appeals and banks of phoners,
All candidates looked urgently for donors.
Yes, raising funds became the salient factor,
And Clinton, given all those cats who backed her,
Was thought to have the edge in doing that.
She'd take the lead, 'twas thought, right off the bat.

Thoughts of Hillary Clinton's Competitors as They Look Forward, with Some Trepidation, to Her First-Quarter Fund-Raising Report

Though Hillary's funders are richer than Croesus,
We hope their largesse toward her cause just decreases.
Perhaps overconfident that she's ahead,
They'll donate their dough to the Red Cross instead.
We hope that each person who does want to fund'll
Just fund by himself, then, and not in a bundle.

Yes, all those candidates who hoped to thwart her
Sure hoped when she reported her first quarter,
Her total might be less than would impress
The party that she surely did possess
The power to become the nominee.
She led the field, but not to the degree
Competitors had feared, and, truth to tell,
Barack Obama'd done almost as well.
The two of them and Edwards did the best;
Those three were seen as having passed the test.
And on the other side, the GOP
Cash grabbers also ended up with three:
Obtaining what contenders must obtain
Were Giuliani, Romney, and McCain.
McCain had spent a lot. His merry band

Had relatively little cash on hand.
Though Rudy finished second raising jack,
The polls still showed him leader of the pack.
Since polls showed Clinton also in the lead,
New Yorkers said it's possible that we'd
Have no one in the race from out of town—
A sort of Subway Series for the crown.
If Bloomberg joined the race for *chef d'état,*
New York would have a, well, *ménage à trois.*

9

Republicans, All Shook Up

By summertime, McCain's campaign was limping.
The cause? In part, his staff was hardly scrimping.
On salaries, hotels, and fancy mailers,
They'd spent this pilot's funds like drunken sailors.
So dough ran low, and some observers spoke
Of chances that McCain's camp could go broke.
And, also, party voters got the vapors
From where John stood on migrants lacking papers.
He didn't advocate we send them packing,
And that had cost him quite a bit of backing—
Except with business types, who saw our neighbor
Providing tons of cheap, nonunion labor.

Back Where You Came From

*(A nativist ballad to twelve million undocumented immigrants,
sung to the tune of "Look to the Rainbow")*

You have broken our law,
So you'll have to go now.
We will move you all out, and I don't care just how.
As for scrubbing our floors
And for picking our crops,
We will figure that out. I'm now calling the cops.

Go back, back where you came from.
Your kind's not wanted; you cannot stay here.
Go back, back where you came from.
I'll mow my own lawn. Just cross that frontier.
I'll clean my own house. Just cross that frontier.

The speculation was that, turn or not,
John wouldn't get the GOP's top spot.
McCain's campaign, some said, was now succumbing,
As if he were Ed Muskie's second coming.
In polls, still, Giuliani held the lead.
His liberal social views did not impede
His cause with Christian Rightists, so it seemed.
In time, in fact, this pro-choice mayor was deemed
Deserving of Pat Robertson's own blessing—

Pat being someone who was filmed expressing
The view that 9/11 was God's way
To tell us not to tolerate what's gay.

Pat Robertson, Protector of Traditional
Family Values, Endorses Rudy Giuliani,
a Serial Adulterer, Who's Pro-choice and
Does Not Think That People Accepting of Gays
Should Be Destroyed by Hurricanes
or Other Disasters

Do politics mandate strange bedfellows? Sure.
So Pat's for a person whose views he'd disparage.
Yes, politics mandate strange bedfellows—sure.
However, where Rudy's concerned, so does marriage.

And Romney also showed consistent strength.
This candidate would go to any length
To show his pro-choice views of yore were gone
And that he would have never had his lawn
Maintained or even on occasion mown
By people lacking papers if he'd known.
His speech is crisp, and he enunciates.
Because of that, he did well in debates.
The first debate took place in Simi Valley.
It sounded like a Ronald Reagan rally.

Each speaker said that Reagan was revered,
And saw himself as Reagan reappeared.
By all these would-be Reagans, surveys stressed,
The Iowans were mostly unimpressed.

Disappointment in Iowa

> Just 19 percent of likely GOP caucus attendees said they were
> "very satisfied" with the field of candidates.
>
> —*The Washington Post*
> August 5, 2007

Though Romney—Flawlessman—is in the lead,
So polished that he might not sweat or bleed,
The average Iowa voter sometimes balks
At voting for a mannequin that talks.
And John McCain—yes, he of straight-talk fame—
Seems much too willing now to play the game.
He felt the call of Falwell and he went;
Since then, his straight talk seems a little bent.
And Giuliani, who derives his powers
From terrorists' destruction of the towers?
The stories of his married life confirm
That, if we can be frank, the man's a worm.
Republicans, the pollsters say, are not
So happy with the candidates they've got.
Some shrinks might say when shove now comes to push,
They're simply yearning to retain George Bush.

10

Huckabee, Rising

Debating for the GOP were ten
Quite serious-looking darkly suited men.
The space among the candidates was tight,
Since all of them were squeezing to the right.
They'd all assert their faith, for attribution,
And three of them rejected evolution.
It is, those three contenders would agree,
Mere theory—and unproved by Charlie D.

On Three Out of the Ten Republican Presidential Candidates Stating That They Don't Believe in Evolution

They think that Darwin's got it wrong:
God made us all. Pow! Just like that.
It could be worse. We still don't know
How many think the Earth is flat.

One man who'd dissed old Darwin in debate
Was Huckabee, best known for how much weight
He'd managed to get rid of with his diet
And how he'd urged Arkansans all to try it.
Though Huckabee thought gayness wasn't wrought
By God, and he believed what's usually taught
By right-wing pastors, Mike, in a debate
Seemed filled with human kindness, not with hate.
His clothes reflected Sears and not Armani.
He didn't snarl like Rudy Giuliani.

The Nicest Republican

The nice vote goes to Huckabee.
No other is as nice as he.
He leads a decent sort of life.
He's married to his only wife.
His kids, we'd bet, still speak to him.
He's courteous, but isn't prim.
A cheerful fat man who got lean,
He'd not vindictive, rude, or mean.
Of course, he thinks our way's been lost:
Abortion is a "holocaust"
And evolution's just a myth.
(The apes are not his kin nor kith;
He knows a human couldn't be
Descended from a chimpanzee.)
And what the Bible says is true.
The Earth's not old. It's rather new—
Six thousand years, from Eve to present.
He's wacko, yes, but he's sure pleasant.

Though Huckabee had little in his kitty
Compared with his opponents, he was witty,
And just as Christian as a man can be.
If there could be a dark horse, why not he?

Bare-Bones Huckabee Creeps Up on Free-Spending Romney in Iowa, While Humming "O Tannenbaum"

Mike Huckabee, Mike Huckabee,
Your numbers just keep soaring.
Mike Huckabee, Mike Huckabee,
It's Romney you are goring,
Though Mitt is rich and Mitt is slick.
He's wondering, "Who is this hick?"
Mike Huckabee, compared with thee,
Mitt Romney is so boring.

11

Democrats in Iowa

Intense campaigning, starting in that spring,
Did not change what 'twas thought the end would bring.
Ms. Clinton, many said, could not be blocked.
Most polls and pols agreed she had it locked.
She came across as well prepared and bright.
She knew the issues as a staffer might.
When asked, the Democrats would tend to rate her
Among them all the very best debater.
Her husband, Bill, rhetorically endowed,
Was with her and could always wow a crowd.
She led the field by plenty nationwide,
But first she'd face the first state to decide,
And that state held for her no guarantee.
Barack was strong, and, as for Edwards, he
Was doing well on issues such as health
And pounding malefactors of great wealth.

Though Dodd's and Biden's efforts weren't igniting,
Some voters found Bill Richardson exciting.
This fellow's résumé is hardly schleppy,
And he's Latino, though his name sounds preppy.
Of leaders in the nominating fight,
Just one was male and Protestant and white.
The other three—and this was not unspoken—
Would face a barrier that had not been broken.

The Democrats More or Less Ignore Senators Joe Biden and Christopher Dodd

Biden and Dodd, Biden and Dodd—
Respectable senators, peas in a pod.
With Bush's side weakened—no, reeling, by God—
You might think it strange and you might think it odd
That, rather than look for some WASP nest to prod,
Some untested, land-mine-laced new ground to trod,
The Democrats simply would now give the nod
To some proven white guy like Biden or Dodd
And win all the votes from Eugene to Cape Cod.
But then they wouldn't be Democrats.

The others? Mike Gravel, who seemed to revel
In being just a bubble off of level,
And also, running hard with perseverance,
A smallish, left-wing man whose frail appearance
Suggested he'd not finished all his spinach.
This was the vegan congressman, Kucinich.

←———————→

12

Still Iowa: Finally, Some Voting

Mitt Romney bet his bucks (he has a few)
On caucuses, where he thought he would do
Quite well, because of all the dough he spent
And how he seemed so eager to repent
Those Massachusetts views he once embraced—
The views that had been totally replaced
By views designed to make a case and vector it
Directly to the heart of this electorate.

Mitt Romney as Doll

*Yes, Mitt's so slick of speech and slick of garb, he
Reminds us all of Ken, of Ken and Barbie—*

So quick to shed his moderate regalia,
He may, like Ken, be lacking genitalia.

But even as Mitt's moderation faded,
The evangelicals were not persuaded.
The man espousing virtues they hold dear
Was Huckabee, and he did sound sincere.
And then he won: the voters liked his style.
The party bigwigs smiled a nervous smile.

GOP Big-Money Bosses Contemplate the Possibility of Going into the General Election with Mike Huckabee as Their Standard-Bearer

We value all the preachers and their flocks.
For them our party platform is designed.
But having someone such as that in charge
Is not exactly what we had in mind.

We really sort of think of them as troops
With whom our interests always are entwined.
But putting one of those types at the top
Is not exactly what we had in mind.

When Democratic caucuses occurred
The world was shocked, for Hillary was third.
Barack had won, and what he had to say
In victory just blew the crowd away.
He said the time had come, that change was here.
In contrast, Clinton's crowd seemed yesteryear.
Obama's future now looked awfully bright—
And partly 'cause he'd won a state that's white.
On TV then, the Sabbath gasbags who'd
Said Hillary was certain didn't brood
About that error. No, as if on cue,
They simply said that Hillary was through.
They said that hopes for her did not remain—
The same thing they had said about McCain.

The Sabbath Gasbags Reconsider Hillary Clinton's Inevitability

*The winner for certain was what she was called
By gasbags until, in the caucus, she stalled.
The gasbags predict now her certain defeat.
For large bags, they're really quite quick on their feet.*

The gasbags, Clinton said, were just dead wrong.
To use the lyrics of an old and treasured song,
She said for her this wasn't such a blues day,
And Super Tuesday would be her good news day.

13

Strategic Thinkers

Like Hillary, who kept on thinking it's
All riding on a Super Tuesday blitz,
Each candidate was following a plan—
Some strategy that varied man to man.
Mitt Romney's plan, which Huckabee had thwarted,
Was win in Iowa and, thus supported,
Expect New Hampshire neighbors then to vote
For him. He'd win, and that'd be all she wrote—
Unless that way of looking at the map
Meant falling into Giuliani's trap.
For Giuliani's strategy was this:
Give early contests more or less a miss.
He'd husband his resources with the thought
That, playing to his strength, he simply ought
To concentrate on Florida, for there
He knew he'd kick collective *derrière*.

The Voters Rudy Giuliani Hopes
to Attract in Florida

A lot of New Yorkers now taking their ease
Recall, when their city was having a crise,
That Rudy, the crime buster, rescued Manhattan.
(Forgotten: the role of his top cop, Bill Bratton.
A part of the story that Rudy would edit
Is firing Bill when the press gave Bill credit.)
Yes, Rudy's the hero they'd name in a quiz.
So they might support him still, worm that he is.

This strategy had left pros so amused
That "cockamamie" was the word they used.
They said by hanging back he'd surely cede
The coverage he'd need to keep his lead.
They said he'd fall too far behind his foes.
At last, for once, the pros were on the nose.
Some other factors did come into play:
For one, a smallish scandal on the way
The city in its debit ledger lists
Security for Giuliani's trysts.
And Bernie Kerik, Rudy's choice to be
Commissioner of cops in NYC—
A man whom Rudy'd rescued from obscurity
And touted to be head of fed security—

Had been indicted, causing some to write,
"At judging people, Rudy's out of sight."
Yes, other factors did come into play,
But, still, it seems appropriate to say
That, given what the strategy produced,
Well, "cockamamie" was the *mot* quite *juste*.

14

Coming Out of Iowa

The Iowa results were a surprise
On both sides, since the winners were two guys
Who hadn't been the favorites at the start.
The race became much harder now to chart.

Two Good Talkers

Obama and Huckabee aren't much alike,
But both can perform well in front of a mike.
As president, either would leave no doubt whether
He's able to string more than six words together.
Their wins may owe something to this expertise:
Articulate presidents don't grow on trees.

The buzz now said that Hillary was through.
For John McCain such talk was nothing new.
In Iowa, his jokes seemed not so funny.
He hadn't even finished in the money.
McCain's campaign again was in a crunch,
Which made the right-wing preachers pleased as punch.

Sweet Jesus, We Hate Him a Lot
(*A hymn of thanksgiving sung by right-wing preachers
about John McCain*)

Oh, thank you, sweet Jesus,
Oh, thank you so much
For any distress John has got.
We hope he continues
This streak of bad luck.
Though Christians, we hate him a lot.

Yes, we hate him a lot, we hate him a lot.
Sweet Jesus, we hate him a lot.

He called us all bigots,
Or something like that.
And just 'cause we slandered his daughter.
We did it for Jesus,
Like all that we do,
And John McCain knows that, or oughter.

Yes, we hate him a lot, we hate him a lot.
Sweet Jesus, we hate him a lot.

He treats us real nice now.
He panders to us.
We know, though, he's not born again.
We hope that he loses.
We'd even prefer
A heathenish Mormon. Amen.

New Hampshire loomed, just five days down the road.
The caucus losers bore a heavy load.
Mike Huckabee, by winning, had Big Mo,
So it was left to Romney's camp to show
That where the neighbors knew him he'd excel—
Unless, of course, they knew him all too well.
Obama, pundits said, had Big Mo, too—
The sort that Hillary could not undo.
But voters in New Hampshire would confound
Them all by turning everything around.
Yes, Hillary won big. Some said the key
Was visual—the tape that showed when she
Explained, while coming very close to tears,
Why, though exhausted, she just perseveres.
Surprisingly, she stole Obama's thunder.
Her camp said he was just a one-hit wonder.
The Sabbath gasbags more or less concurred.
They said Obamamania was cured.

McCain had won, and kept his cause from dying.
So it was Romney's folks who did the crying.
Fred Thompson, heir to Reagan, had so far
Just failed to demonstrate he was a star.
A puzzled look remained upon his face,
And he declined to keep a rapid pace.
He'd started late, and hadn't closed the gap—
Most Reaganesque in that he liked his nap.
As Carolina focused the campaign,
The short odds were on Clinton and McCain—
The very people all had talked about
Before this lengthy process started out.

15

South Carolina: The Field Narrows

The contests served their purpose of depleting
The field of candidates who were competing.
Chris Dodd and Joseph Biden chose to join
In dropping out quite early, in Des Moines.
For Richardson, the Granite State was hard.
He hacked away, but couldn't chip a shard.
So he dropped out. His colleagues called, of course,
To pay respects and see whom he'd endorse.
His blessing wouldn't simply soothe one's ego:
Latino votes might flow to his amigo.
For Thompson, Carolina was the test
On whither went his presidential quest.
The pros said, "That's a state he has to take,
And he just might, if he can stay awake."
In Carolina, though, he'd have to fight
With Huckabee for voters on the Right.

For John McCain this state recalled the time
He got shot down again, this time with slime—
With phony push-polls seeking to besmirch
And lying leaflets handed out in church.
Eight years had passed. He'd tried to make his peace.
He hoped the gutter tactics there would cease—
No spreading rumors by Rove's slimy creatures,
And no un-Christian treatment from the preachers.

Progress from the 2000 Campaign of George W. Bush in South Carolina

Well, nobody seems to be sliming so far.
John says to the preachers, "I'm holy as thou."
It's possible no one will ask him at all
"So where's that black love child of yours living now?"

The slurring, it appeared, this time was checked.
John's pandering, perhaps, had some effect.
It wasn't just the preachers he had soothed;
The rough bumps with his party had been smoothed.
McCain now said that he would always fight
The immigration bill that he helped write.
On torture and on tax cuts for the rich
He'd found it in his heart to make a switch.

His stark survival verdict had been rendered:
On nearly every issue he surrendered.
And he did win. Fred Thompson's finish meant
That it was time for Fred to fold his tent.
Yes, Fred got out, but evidence was thin
That he was there when he said he was in.
The Democrats had turned a trifle mean,
Especially when Bill Clinton made the scene.

A Democratic Primary Version of "Hickory Dickory Dock"

Hillary, dillary dock.
Hil ran into Barack.
So Bill got shrill
Defending Hil.
Hillary, dillary dock.

Some African Americans were peeved,
For Bill had played the race card, they believed.
Bill begged to differ, and he kept on yakking.
It often was Barack he was attacking,
And, sometimes, in a casual remark, he
Began to sound, some thought, a little snarky.
Obama won, and that's when things got messy:

Essentially, Bill said, "Well, so did Jesse."
Some pundits wrote that Hil's campaign might fare
A little better if Bill wasn't there.

He's Still My Bill

(*A reprise of the* Show Boat *classic as sung by Hillary Clinton after the South Carolina primary*)

Along came Bill.
He wouldn't shut his trap.
He yammered at the church
And at the shopping mall.
He tried to knock
And mock Barack.
And all that palaver
Just turned off the voters.
But I will not say, "Oh, Bill, please stay away."
He just may still
Draw voters my way in Super Tuesday's votes.
If so, he's still my Bill.

16

Just the Two of Us

John Edwards, placing third again, was out.
That left his side a two-contender bout.
Of hard-fought Democratic fights of yore,
It most resembled nineteen eighty-four.
Each candidate appeared to have a part:
Yes, she played Mondale. He played Gary Hart.
Experience was what Fritz Mondale stressed.
It's what he said that he, not Hart, possessed—
The knowledge that the White House would demand,
So when he got there he could take command.
And if the red phone rang, he said, you know
Which one of us you'd want to say "Hello."

A Short Poem on the Issues
by Hillary Clinton

The issue is clear,
So I can be brief:
I'm ready to be
Commander in chief.

Obama's rhetoric, she said, was lofty
But unsubstantial air, like Mister Softee,
Unanchored to the details it omits—
Precisely what was said of Hart by Fritz.

Another, Slightly Longer, Poem by
Hillary Clinton, This Time on Barack Obama

His rhetoric's soaring,
Defying belief.
But what's there behind it?
Yes, where is the beef?

> *Yes, where is the beef?*
> *His hand on the tiller*
> *Would mean we'd be fed*
> *A diet of filler.*

Experience, Obama said, was nice,
But seasoning alone does not suffice,
And, given some decisions Clinton made,
It's clear that wisdom's not just time in grade.
For if it truly were, why did she back
George Bush's mad adventure in Iraq?
(If time in government can make one brainy,
Explain the role of Rumsfeld and of Cheney.)
He sounded as if Clinton were a part
Of bygone ways from which he would depart
When government was something he controlled,
And he swept in the new, swept out the old.
On issues, these two didn't differ greatly;
They both were slightly to the Left, innately.
And so they circled, always very wary
Of gaffes, while she played Fritz and he played Gary.
They both thought one would score a solid win
As soon as Super Tuesday's votes were in.
When Super Tuesday came, though, by and by,
It turned out to be more or less a tie.
And after Super Tuesday, he kept winning,
Which made it hard for her to go on spinning

A tale that showed her somehow out in front.
So she and her campaign became quite blunt
About Obama's weakness and their hunch
Republicans would have this guy for lunch.

Thou Not So Swell

(*Sung to the tune of Rodgers and Hart's "Thou Swell" by
Hillary Clinton to Barack Obama*)

You're still untested.
I've been around.
I'm here. I'm vested.
I'm not newfound.
You are undefined, and
Wet behind the ears.
I've been putting together arcane legislation for years.
Though crowds go crazy to hear you speak.
Your meaning's hazy, and not unique.
You are just a rock star,
One whose flocks are bound
To dissolve. You're trendy. I'm sound.

17

Obama, Descending

McCain seemed, after Super Tuesday, set—
No longer facing any serious threat.
Though Romney and Mike Huckabee remained,
The energy of their campaigns had waned.

Mitt Romney, the PowerPoint Moneybag, Will Stay in the Race

Though Romney seems beaten he vows to press on.
He'll battle McCain, he has said, till the last.
He'll spend yet more money for ads on TV—
A stimulus package that he alone passed.

As things turned out, Mike Huckabee stayed longer,
Though his campaign was hardly getting stronger.
Republicans and Democrats alike
Had found that they were rather soft on Mike.
And so, when, finally, he departed, too,
The folks on both sides bid a fond adieu.

Democrats Say Farewell to Mike Huckabee

Oh, sure, your policies regarding
Taxation sound like Warren Harding.
But you're so nice, Mike Huckabee,
That even liberals such as we
Forgive you that, y mucho más:
Your Bible thumper's mishegoss.
Mike Huckabee, we wish you'd won,
Since you're the only one who's fun,
The only one whose campaign jokes
Did not seem wrought by other folks.
We wish you'd won, Mike, most of all
'Cause we could beat you in the fall.

The Clinton camp, so confident she'd romp
On Super Tuesday, sank now in a swamp.
Her leading lights were stumped on what to try:

They'd had one plan and it had gone awry.
It seemed Barack Obama might be able
In early springtime tests to run the table.
But, just as he seemed headed for the throne,
Barack ran into troubles of his own.
Yes, something changed the campaign overnight:
The very Reverend Jeremiah Wright.
Obama's pastor, Wright expressed his ire
With lots of brimstone and a touch of fire.
Like Robertson, he'd said that 9/11
Was punishment, sent here by God from heaven.
But he thought that those horrible attacks
Were punishment for how we'd treated blacks.
And someone with a camera saw him say
That we should say "God damn the USA."
Thus Reverend Wright was bearded in his den:
The dreaded YouTube camera'd struck again.

YouTube
(*Sung this time to the tune of "Blue Moon"
by the Reverend Jeremiah Wright*)

YouTube
I saw you out on patrol.
But I continued to rant.
That's me when I'm on a roll.

YouTube
All the computers now show me.
Barack would like to flambeau me.
He may just have to heave-ho me.

And then, verily, I got invited
To Washington to give a talk.
I said some things that got them more excited.
And after that, Barack said, "Take a walk!"

YouTube
I saw you out on patrol.
But I continued to rant.
That's me when I'm on a roll.

Obama then spoke movingly on race.
His eloquence for some could not erase
His longtime closeness with the Reverend Wright—
Chicago years Obama still stayed tight
With someone who could damn the USA.
And what, these people said, did that convey
About a candidate who—all knew well—
Did not display a flag on his lapel?
Could someone with a background so exotic
Be really, truly, red-blood patriotic?

Patriotism 2008

I backed the war in Nam, okay,
Though I used pull to stay away.
A patriot? But can't you tell?
I wear a flag on my lapel.

My company's now based offshore;
We don't pay taxes anymore.
A patriot? But can't you tell?
I wear a flag on my lapel.

That clean-air stuff's not meant for me.
I drive a German SUV.
A patriot? But can't you tell?
I wear a flag on my lapel.

We needn't build a grand memorial
To patriots. It's all sartorial.

Another gift that Reverend Wright presented
Obamaphobes was that his words augmented
The notion that, despite Barack's life story,
He wasn't in that special category
Of black folks white folks don't consider black—
The breed apart from Jesse Jackson's claque.

One reason they obsessed on Wright's transgression
Was that it let them further an impression:
Barack's as close to Wright as cheek to jowl,
So he's not Tiger Woods nor Colin Powell.
Since no one thought his cause would show improvement
If he became connected with the movement,
There was a racial subtext to this spat:
Barack is black, and militant at that.

A Citizen Who Has Tried to Keep Informed Addresses Those Covering the 2008 Presidential Election

I'm now opposed to Reverend Wright.
I don't support him anymore.
I only have one question left:
Just what's the reverend running for?

18

$\longleftrightarrow$

I Won't Quit. Don't Ask Me.

Before they'd end the Fritz and Gary Show,
They had a lot of contests yet to go—
Their fight now less like Mondale versus Hart
Than World War I, the long trench warfare part.
(The similarity was not mysterious:
No movement, and the casualties were serious.)

Competition

Hamas is for Barack, so said McCain.
Old John, Barack replied, must be confused.
McCain, though, showed his sharpness in a way:
He found a knock the Clintons hadn't used.

Obama now was in the lead, but just,
And as they moved to states best known for rust,
The voters to whom Clinton held on tight
Had collars that were blue but skin quite white.
They were, she said to anyone she met,
The voters that Barack could never get.
For Democrats, the case she tried to make
Was that she'd win the states they had to take.
It's true she won such states against Barack,
Except the delegates she added to her stock
Compared to his were not in an amount
To alter what might be the final count.
(The superdelegates, once votes were in,
Would likely go with who they thought would win.)
Those counting delegates were all aware
The math for Hillary was just not there.
But Clinton said the race was still quite close,
And, close or not, she wouldn't say adios.
She said she wouldn't buckle, fold, or bend.
The role of a contender's to contend.
The Clinton team, an often squabbling crew,
Considered "quit" a word that was taboo.
The drumbeat played by Hillary stayed steady:
She said Barack Obama wasn't ready.
But others in the party were beginning
To say that Hillary had had her inning.
Since her attacks, they thought, could never save her,
They only did Republicans a favor.
By saying he can't win she was distilling
A prophecy that might be self-fulfilling.

On the Struggle for the Democratic Nomination

Top Democrats now want to shout,
"Oh Hillary, please just get out!"
But Hillary and Bill still say,
"Get out? Give up? Slink off? No way."

What's left? To wound Barack, thus drain
His numbers vis-à-vis McCain,
Then say, "He's eloquent and all,
But damaged. He can't win this fall."

Republicans seemed sunk before—
A grim economy, the war.
But now the Democrats make news:
They've figured out a way to lose.

In May, she said she planned to run some more,
Although Tim Russert, he who kept the score
Of how the delegates were now divided,
Announced the end had plainly been decided.
On NBC's *Today,* he told the host
That Hillary's campaign at last was toast.
The Sabbath gasbags then began to mention
The chance she'd stage a fight at the convention.
But then in June her fans began their grieving,

'Cause Hillary announced that she was leaving.
Yes, Hillary stepped up in June and said
She'd stop her quest, and back Barack instead.
She swallowed, with a smile, this bitter pill.
It wasn't clear the same was true of Bill.

The Melody Hillary Clinton Finally Heard
(*As sung, by a brave staffer, to the tune of "The Party's Over"*)

This race is over.
You lost the delegate count.
And it was March, by the way,
When math showed his lead too large to surmount.
It's time to shut down your big machine.
So just endorse him. And try not sounding mean.

This race is over.
Well, yes, that's hard to accept.
They thought you'd win in a walk,
And who could expect a staff that inept?
It's time to stop now. And try stopping Bill.
It's all over, my friend.

19

Presumptive and Impure

With all the party contests finally through,
The first thing for a nominee to do
Is downplay certain views so that his bid'll
Attract the voters clustered in the middle.
(Until that day, so many of his pledges
Are custom-made for voters at the edges.)
But some Obama followers were sure
That doing so would make him less than pure—
Or maybe just as evil as Iago.
(Who might not seem that evil in Chicago,
Whose pols were studied by the young Barack
As they sewed up each precinct block by block.)
Like Clinton diehards spoiling for a row,
These purists told Barack they might say ciao.

Obama and the Purists

They said, "You were our hero, fresh and glistening,
Barack, you were our idol and you fell."
"I'm just the same," he said. "You've not been listening."
They said, "We note a flag on your lapel."

McCain's campaign's impurity was based
On all the lobbyists whom he embraced.
For years, as senator, McCain had ranted
About the influence that they've been granted.
Yet his campaign was thought of as uncanny
For having them in every nook and cranny.
At last, McCain said he was throwing out
The ones about whose clout there was a doubt.

McCain and Lobbyists

The working lobbyists in his campaign,
Says now-and-then reformer John McCain,
And those receiving any of their pay
From foreign sources have to go away.
That surely could reduce the payroll's heft:
It's possible he'll have no staffers left.

Deciding just to whom this rule applies
Is someone who's a lobbyist. Surprise!
Will doing what the candidate's desiring
Necessitate an act of auto-firing?

Both candidates, as their campaigns changed missions,
Had modified some strongly held positions.
Obama now said he thought he was willing
To see a little bit of offshore drilling.
Their campaigns' cultures, though, were not the same.
The bosses of McCain's would try to maim
Each other as they fought like dogs and cats,
With whispered knocks in off-the-record chats.
Barack Obama's camp seemed more controlled.
Its people mostly did what they were told.

Management Styles

McCain's operation is seat-of-the-pants,
With rivalries, arguments, grudges, and rants.
Obama's campaign is more corporate and smooth—
No fights at the top and few egos to soothe.
Political junkies say something's unclear:
Just who in the hell's the Republican here?

20

Defining

The strategy is old: You must define
Your rival first, as somehow not benign.
Barack? The GOP implied that he
Was something other—not like you and me.
The right-wing blogs invented facts about him
Designed to cause Americans to doubt him:
A terrorist who's playing us for fools?
At least a guy who went to Muslim schools?
(McCain helped out. One slur that he disbursed:
Obama doesn't put his country first.)
This didn't start with right-wing blogs. No, when
The Clinton camp competed, one Mark Penn—
Who's much like Rove, except he always loses—
Was busy telling those with whom he schmoozes
Barack's no real American at all,
And thus would be defeated in the fall.

On Mark Penn's Deciding Who Has "Fundamentally American Roots" and Who Doesn't

Obama is not an authentically true
American, so says Mark Penn in his writing.
If Penn is the model to which we must hew,
It makes being foreign sound rather inviting.

To raise more doubts about Obama's life,
The right wing turned its spotlight on his wife.

A Smear-Cheer for Michelle Obama
(As performed by the Swiftboat Singers)

Who's not a retiring, shy Southern belle?
Whose Harvard degree is the way you can tell
That she's so elite she once ate a morel?
Who doesn't wear flag pins on either lapel?
Michelle.
Rah! Rah! Smear! Rah! Rah!

Who might be a part of a terrorist cell?
Who might have the powers for casting a spell?
Whose fist-knocks may summon the devil from hell?

> *Who could be, we reckon, a Muslim as well?*
> *Michelle.*
> *Rah! Rah! Smear! Rah! Rah!*

The Democrats' one overarching aim?
Maintain McCain and Bush are just the same.
To vote McCain, they said, was to confirm
George W. for yet another term.
For all his maverick talk, they said that he
Was, in his heart, the same as Forty-three.
For John McCain, Bush Two was Reverend Wright,
And that presented John with quite a plight:
His base made him unwilling to disgorge
All links that tied him tightly to our George.
On Bush's war, he said the surge's gain
Means victory if our troops can remain.
Security for him was at the fore.
He said that he and not Barack knew war
And how to win a war at any cost.
(Although the one that he was in we lost.)

21

World Tour

McCain maintained Obama was still green:
He'd judged the war although he'd barely seen
The situation firsthand on the ground,
So he should make the trip and hang around.
Obama did, and playing with GIs,
He sank a shot that came to symbolize
The trip—a soaring set shot being tried
By someone new who's shooting from outside.
Iraq's PM said (getting out of line)
Barack's plan for withdrawal sounds just fine.
The photo ops with brass had great potential
For showing him as being presidential.
In Europe, he met Brown and he met Merkel,
Who seemed to welcome him into their circle—
A circle some said Bush had all but closed.
And Sarkozy? He practically proposed.

Barack drew crowds, especially in Berlin.
(Most Europeans wanted him to win.)
McCain's camp roundly mocked Obama's throngs.
They said no U.S. candidate belongs
In foreign settings, treated like a star,
With homeland problems being what they are.

What the McCain Campaign Seems to Be Saying About Obama's Trip Abroad

Obama's rock-star tour is done.
The foreign cheering has abated.
Unseemly's what we thought it was.
We'd like a president who's hated.

Great adulation from abroad
Should not by presidents be prized.
We are the leaders of the world.
Our president should be despised.

It's better when he's thought to be
A threat to peace and rather slow,
When animosity's so strong
There're many places he can't go.

> *Then he can say to leaders when*
> *There's something that we hope they'll do,*
> *"Associate yourself with me*
> *And you, then, can be hated too."*

McCain's folks slammed Obama for his fame—
An echo of how Rove had played the game.
The last change in McCain's campaign had brought
Some Rove-o-Clones who followed what he taught:
To maim your rival, go to any length
Attacking not his weakness but his strength.
(A hero's smeared by people working for
A man whose clout had kept him out of war.)
And now the Rove-o-Clones were in John's pay,
And, judging from the ads, they had their way.

How the Rove-o-Clones Would Have Conducted an Election Campaign Against Nelson Mandela

> *This prison time Nelson Mandela bemoans—*
> *Those years spent in labor like breaking up stones—*
> *Were really not nearly as grim as you'd think.*
> *There're many worse ways to do time in the clink.*
> *Yes, sure, he broke stones. That is no real surprise.*

But fewer, we hear, than did some other guys.
With that lovely climate, how bad could it be?
It wasn't for life or he wouldn't be free.
So calling it martyrdom really is stretching.
A few years in prison is no cause for kvetching.
He won the Nobel, yes, but so did some Reds—
Some people who'd murder us all in our beds.
How odd that he's honored in such far-off regions
(*The Nobel's the prize of a bunch of Norwegians*).
To win this election is now his priority.
So spare us that bit about moral authority.

22

So Where's the Blowout?

The prospects for the GOP looked dim
Before the credit crisis got so grim
That economic sages weren't averse
To saying things were bad and could get worse.
McCain had said forthrightly all along
His grasp of economics wasn't strong.
McCain's main man on economic matters
Said our economy was not in tatters.
The problem was, he said, our point of view,
And that's been whiny rather than can-do.

Phil Gramm Says We're a Nation of Whiners

As senator, Phil was among the designers
Of laws that helped Enron, which showed no decliners,
Manipulate prices of oil from refiners.
(Its stock can be used in your cat box, for liners.)
His laws helped the mortgage thieves rook naïve signers
Who then lost their houses and can't afford diners.
So now he decides we're a nation of whiners.
Figures.

Recession and Obama's boffo trip
Would, pundits thought, permit Barack to zip
At once into a double-digit lead.
So when that didn't happen they decreed
His lead should now be twice as large at least.
And that decree eventually released
Hot air on cable news and Sunday shows
On why he led McCain by just a nose:
His small lead shows (just how they don't reveal)
That he's a guy who still can't close the deal.
This subject would have lasted them for weeks
Except they started analyzing leaks
About which veep each candidate would choose,
And whether that would help him win or lose.
For John McCain they made a lengthy list,

Including a Floridian named Crist.
(Since Charlie Crist's so well regarded there,
They'd win the state, but this time fair and square.)
Pols mentioned Graham, Portman, Sanford, Thune—
And Romney, panting in the wings since June.
On Lieberman, ur-Christians had to warn
That, since Joe's not concerned with the unborn,
His pick could mean to delegates that they
Were serving Jesus if they voted nay.
The same was true of Ridge: Abortion foes
Had told McCain they'd greet that choice with no's.
So, operating in a smaller tent, he
Might turn, some thought, to Governor Pawlenty.
The Democratic list was just as thick,
Since no one knew just how Obama'd pick
His veep. Would he choose someone who might try
To turn a red state blue, like Evan Bayh?
Or would Obama's narrow lead now widen
If he chose some old hand—let's say Joe Biden
Or Richardson—who as a running mate
Could bring to foreign policy some weight.
(Bill's beard was like some dude's from Portofino,
But he had heft, and he was still Latino.)
And, meanwhile, Democrats, who'd seemed so slack
In answering the Rove-o-Clones' attack,
Now said that John McCain was out of touch
With ordinary people, inasmuch
As, asked how many premises he had,
He didn't know. It sounded rather bad:

On houses, John McCain, when asked his views,
Was like Imelda asked about her shoes.

The Rime of the Ancient Candidate
(*John McCain adapts Samuel Coleridge's epic*)

You'd know at once that I am not
Some liberal elitist.
I'm just a beer-and-burger guy
Who finds a cookout neatest.

Unlike Barack, I wouldn't eat
Arugula instead.
So what if I'm a little long
On spots to lay my head?

Houses, houses everywhere,
Not one of them a shack—
So many it's not strange I have
Some trouble keeping track.

Houses, houses everywhere—
Abodes in the amount
No short-term memory's involved
In failing to keep count.

To folks who fear they'll lose a home
As mortgage markets swerve,
I have some practical advice:
Keep six more in reserve.

23

Denver

Obama folks thought they'd be sitting pretty
When they assembled in the Mile High City.
But, maybe 'cause the air up there's so thin,
They showed some qualms about their chance to win.
As usual in the media profession,
Reporters, in a pack, chose one obsession:
Was Clinton and Obama's pact now sealed,
The bitter feelings of her fans all healed?
The news was full of fall electoral plans
Of those who'd been Ms. Clinton's strongest fans.
Reminded that McCain—pro-life, pro-war—
Opposes all the things they've battled for,
Some said, "At least Obama he is not."
So TV teams all gathered round and shot
The Noseless Diehards going through their paces
(They'd cut their noses off to spite their faces).

The Chant of the Noseless Diehards
(*Accompanied by the Cable News Chorus*)

We're Democrats always, but now we'll endeavor
To sit this one out, or pull John McCain's lever—
Though he's always wrong and he isn't that clever.
We do this to prove, well, to prove, well . . . whatever.

Michelle Obama's speech was thought so stunning
Some pundits said, "A pity she's not running."
Ted Kennedy, despite his own grave plight,
Appeared to cheers for Camelot's last knight.
Mark Warner's keynote failed to make a splash,
He's now got less panache, but still has cash.
Joe Biden, picked for veep, addressed the throng—
But, showing discipline, for not too long.
(Joe carries many thoughts inside his head,
And often leaves but few of them unsaid.)
The Clintons, speaking to the Clinton base,
Quite eloquently made Obama's case:
Bill's pearls of wisdom couldn't have been much pearlier,
Too bad, some said, he hadn't dropped them earlier.
A stadium is where Barack would speak—
A red flag for the GOP critique.
(Great oratory, Rove-o-Clones imply,
Is just an affectation, like some guy

Who went to Harvard or eats foreign food
Or reads a lot or dresses like a dude—
All empty words. Since when's a great oration
Been used to comfort or to stir a nation?)
Most commentators said it was terrific
That in this speech Obama got specific
About the issues and he made it plain
He'd happily send zingers toward McCain.
Despite those things McCain has to his credit,
Obama said, the man just doesn't get it,
And though he likes to play the maverick's game,
He votes with Bush. They are, at base, the same.

A Basketball Scout's Updated Report on Barack Obama

He tries showy triples from way, way downtown.
Those three-pointer types often play with restraint.
But lately his outings have made us believe
He'll do his own shoving when he's in the paint.

Material for the Rove-o-Clones was ample:
Another speech to use as an example
Of blatant acts of eloquence that show
Barack as president's not apropos.

24

St. Paul

At first the great storm Gustav cast a pall:
The news was hardly in St. Paul at all,
But in the Gulf—recalling that grim day
Katrina hit, and Bush was still at play
And didn't seem to notice 'til he found
Illusions of his competence had drowned.
(New Orleans suffered multiple deluges
While Brownie, Bush, and Chertoff played three stooges.)
St. Paul's initial day was cut way back
As Gustav slowly readied his attack.

Disturbing Thought

Coordination happened in advance.
Bush skipped St. Paul, was near the storm's huge eye.
Katrina'd shown the White House crowd as clowns.
With Gustav they were given one more try.

We're all relieved that they've improved their act
(And Gustav weakened as it came onshore).
The implication, though, is rather fraught:
Will they now try to start a better war?

They saw Bush there just briefly on a screen—
About as much of him as they'd want seen.
The leader of the party at convention
Was barely thought deserving of a mention.
What wasn't heard in slogans and in cheers?
Incumbent-party chants like "Four more years."

Conspiracy Theory

They had to ask the president to speak,
Though his approval ratings were so weak
Republicans all whispered in the hall,

"Could he just find some way to skip St. Paul?"
Then, just before the party was to start,
They came up with a course that they could chart.
They telephoned Pat Robertson to say,
"Ask God to send a hurricane today."

McCain, in Dayton, said his number two
Was Sarah Palin. Even pols said, "Who?"
But one group knew enough to show delight:
She was an idol of the Christian Right—
A pro-life zealot, and, no need to say,
Quite born-again and in the NRA.

On Sarah Palin's Revelations of God's Will

A pipeline for natural gas is God's will,
And ditto the war in Iraq, so said she.
And why's she so certain of what God wants done?
'Cause she and the Deity always agree.

So don't be upset if she's president when
The telephone next to her bed rings at three.
She'll know quite precisely just what must be done,
'Cause she and the Deity always agree.

Her story, *Hockey Mom*, had its appeal,
But, mainly, Palin was a way to heal
McCain's old breach with preachers and their crew
Who now said they were for him through and through.
His platform for the race was also striking
In being, more than Bush's, to their liking.
His party was no longer torn asunder,
And all he'd had to do was knuckle under.

Sweet Jesus, We Like Him Much Better

(*A hymn of forgiveness sung by right-wing preachers about John McCain*)

Oh, thank you, sweet Jesus,
Oh, thank you so much.
At last John has learned he's our debtor.
He chose Sarah Palin,
Who's real born-again.
Who cares if his guys didn't vet her?

Yes, we like him much better, we like him much better.
Sweet Jesus, we like him much better.

She wouldn't kill babies,
Which Lieberman's for.
And that's why McCain had to get her.
He listens to us now.

He's up in our laps.
He yelps like a small Irish setter.

Yes, we like him much better, we like him much better.
Sweet Jesus, we like him much better.

And then the press, as is its wont, intruded
To find some facts that hadn't been included:
Reform, McCain had said, was Palin's biggie,
But once she'd been Alaska's earmark piggy.
A multitasking mom to those who'd toast her,
She was, more than a candidate, a poster.
When facts about her family were heard,
The poster-perfect picture got quite blurred.
Republicans, now feeling some duress,
Were blaming the elitist liberal press.
Convention speakers slammed the press with glee,
And then attacked Obama's thin CV.
The Palin speech—her test, it was perceived—
Was well delivered and was well received.
The people in the hall were quite ecstatic,
And impact in the country was dramatic.
She was a star—yes, managing to reach
That special status after just one speech.
(Had anyone done such a thing before?
Well, duh: Barack Obama in '04.)
Republicans said she could not be topped,
As long as stories from Alaska stopped.

Accepting, John McCain insisted change
Was something he and Palin could arrange
In Washington—which was a real disgrace,
Although his party'd lately run the place.
He said that many others were politer,
But he had been, for all his life, a fighter—
A maverick. Indeed, he'd earned that word
'Til, desperate to win, he joined the herd.

25

Sizzle Added

The week that followed, John McCain campaigned
With Sarah Palin, who now doubtless reigned
As flavor of the month, with many cheers—
As celebrated as, well, Britney Spears.
In drawing crowds, this snarky hockey momma
Was turning out to be McCain's Obama.
The crowds she drew were huge and they were wowed.
No questions from the press, though, were allowed:
For that week, as they got her up to speed
By feeding her the factoids she might need,
Ms. Palin was, despite her great appeal,
No more accessible than Kim Jong-il.
And if upon the truth she'd sometimes trample—
About the "bridge to nowhere," for example—
And cause the press to say, upon review,
That what she said was not remotely true,

She'd say it yet again, with no contrition,
As if she'd make it true by repetition.

Truth by Repetition

*(Sarah Palin, via speeches, and the press, via news accounts,
discuss her position on the "bridge to nowhere.")*

*I told them thanks, but no thanks, Palin said.
We'd rather pay for it ourselves instead.*

*But here's a tape on which you clearly say
You're for the bridge. The federals should pay.*

*I told them thanks, but no thanks, Palin said.
We'd rather pay for it ourselves instead.*

*You weren't opposed at all until the day
That Congress made that project DOA.*

*I told them thanks, but no thanks, Palin said.
We'd rather pay for it ourselves instead.*

*And then you thought it perfectly okay
For you to take the money anyway.*

> *I told them thanks, but no thanks, Palin said.*
> *We'd rather pay for it ourselves instead.*
>
> *But . . . oh, skip it.*

Her jolt to the campaign was so galvanic.
It pushed some Democrats quite close to panic.
Though from the start she'd come out in attack,
It wasn't clear how they'd attack her back.
Although the GOP's the party which
Has always carried water for the rich—
The folks with major incomes to dispose,
The country clubbers, and the CEOs
Whose normal way of cheering on the Sox is
To fly their private planes to private boxes—
They've managed to convince folks on the street
It's Democrats who harbor the elite,
And laying down the Sarah Palin card,
Meant critics had to play to this canard.
She styled herself as coming from the masses—
A Harry Truman with more costly glasses.
If you described her CV as a joke,
Then you're some overeducated bloke
Who puts down "small-town values" we hold dear
(And which she'll bring to Washington next year).
If you point out that when she ran Wasilla
She acted less like Truman than Godzilla,
Then you're some Eastern snob who snacks on brie

And doesn't own a gun or ATV.
Her presence on the ticket, though, would force
McCain's campaign to quickly change its course.
"Experience" now couldn't be the claim.
So they just ran, by lowering their aim,
The most distorted ads they could devise.
The *Times* and others called them "flat out lies."
McCain of old would not allow such scat.
His honor meant much more to him than that.
But into Bush's role with Rove he'd slid.
What torture couldn't do, ambition did.

26

Fundamentals

As Rove-o-Clones in deepest mud kept slithering,
The criticism in the press was withering.
McCain's ads, many said, were a disgrace.
The View called him a liar to his face.
At one point, slime-campaigning's reigning star—
Yes, Rove, the master—said they'd gone too far.
(Yes, Rove! That criticism had an echo—
Like being slammed for greed by Gordon Gekko.)
However harshly panned for its invective,
The Rove-o-Clones' attack seemed quite effective:
The ads and Sarah Palin's burst of fame
Put John McCain's campaign back in the game.
Some told Barack, "Attack, for if you tarry
You'll just be buried in the mud, like Kerry."
But Palin didn't long remain the rage.
From Wall Street, rumbling sounds were heard offstage.

The Bush economy in its eighth year
Was causing not just loathing but some fear.
Its fundamentals, said McCain, were *bueno*,
And then it almost blew like a volcano.
The crisis that we'd been assured was past
Was, Paulsen and Bernanke said, so vast
They had to bail out Fannie Mae and Freddie
And AIG, to keep the markets steady
And keep the rot from doing much more harm.
And, meanwhile, Lehman Brothers bought the farm.

John McCain Explains What He Meant by Saying That the Fundamentals of the Economy Are Strong

*The fundamentals are strong, my friends. The
 fundamentals are strong.*
*The Democrats don't go along, my friends, but they're the
 ones who are wrong.*
*Because what that word really means, my friends, is our
 great American workers.*
*So anyone saying I'm wrong, my friends, is saying our
 workers are shirkers.*
*So trust me to sort this all out, my friends. I've been in
 Congress the longest.*
*American workers are strong, my friends. And those in the
 swing states are strongest.*

And there was more: Hank Paulson and his backers
Requested seven hundred billion smackers
To buy whatever he thought needed buying.
(Just Hank. No oversight. No ratifying.)
Both candidates talked oversight. Both chose
To warn against enriching CEOs.
But they seemed strapped for what they really could
Best say about what no one understood.
Yes, gazing now at what the Street had wrought
They must have had some moments when they thought,
"The complication of this stuff recalls
The caucus rules in Ames or Cedar Falls."
One campaign change the crisis did produce:
It buried talk of lipstick and of moose.
When what's at risk is everybody's money,
Just who will be in charge is not so funny.
The issue tilted blue, most pols agreed.
Barack Obama went back in the lead.

27

Movement

The crisis grew, and polls began to show
McCain's campaign no longer had Big Mo.
He'd said that in a crisis action mattered,
But actions that he took seemed rather scattered.
He said the president (near absentee)
Should can the chairman of the SEC—
Although, McCain was told within the hour,
The president does not possess that power.
He said he'd stop campaigning to confront
The crisis, but that seemed more like a stunt.
He'd not debate unless a deal was signed,
He said, but then, again, he changed his mind.
He said his actions got a better bill—
But that's the bill his party was to kill.
Some called Barack too cool. McCain was scrappy.
But scrappy didn't make the voters happy.

(Though coolness has its limitations, it'll
Prevent comparisons with Chicken Little.)
The first debate reflected these same styles;
Obama had the edge, though not by miles.
The pols said for Barack it was a gain
To seem as presidential as McCain.
By then, McCain's advisors had a clue
That picking Palin hadn't been a coup.
Once interviews were present for critiquing,
The Sarah Palin bubble started leaking.
Though no one tried to power fastballs past her,
Her interviews were simply a disaster.
Reviews became especially sulphuric
When Palin had a chat with Katie Couric.
On Russia's being not so far away
She sounded eerily like Tina Fey.

On a Clear Day, I See Vladivostok

(The Barbra Streisand standard as sung by Sarah Palin)

On a clear day
I see Vladivostok,
So I know world affairs.
Don't say, "No way."
Though I know elites mock,
It's osmosis that does it—well, that and our
* prayers.*

And Joe Biden sees New Jersey from his shore.
And that's just a state. That doesn't rate. It's me who
   knows the score.
On a clear day,
On a clear day,
I see Vladivostok . . .
And Novosibirsk . . .
And Krasnoyarsk . . .
And Novokuznetsk . . .
And Omsk . . .
And Tomsk . . .
And more!

Now even some conservatives said she
Was not equipped for prime time in D.C.
But in debate, although quite far from weighty,
She did much better than she'd done with Katie.
In spouting talking points, she wasn't tasked
With answering the question she was asked.
Supporters quickly said that she'd been great.
The slogan they might fashion postdebate
To show it was among her greatest hits
Was "Vote for Palin—Not a Total Ditz."

28

More Movement

Financial news got grimmer every day,
And as it did, Obama pulled away.
Those rooting for McCain were saying, "Wait!
He'll turn this thing around in the debate."
He thrives at town hall talks, so they were betting
He'd clean Obama's clock while in that setting.
But as McCain roamed up and down the stage—
At times, it seemed, suppressing a great rage—
He offered many different themes at random.
(Were he and Wall Street melting down in tandem?)
And minutes after that debate was done,
The instant polling said Obama won.
McCain's advisors flat-out said that they
Would now go negative, and they'd portray
Obama in the past and then discuss
How, truth to tell, he's just not "one of us."

They figured that the answer to their prayers
Might be once-violent radical Bill Ayers,
With whom Obama, plus some CEOs
(Who may themselves be dangerous. Who knows?)
Had worked years back to fund and then extend a
Chicago public-school-reform agenda.
In making this attack, Ms. Palin led.
"He pals around with terrorists," she said.

Someone Watching Sarah Palin's Campaign Speeches Imagines How She Might Challenge a Referee's Call in a Sixth-Grade Hockey Game

HOCKEY MOM:
But ref, that's a goal that cannot be okayed.
Remember the spitball that in second grade
Caromed off the teacher's nose? This little bird
Was close with the thrower, or that's what I heard.

REFEREE:
The puck's in the net, and when that's where it lands,
The only call possible's "Johnny's goal stands."

HOCKEY MOM:
They rode the same school bus—yes, he and that thug.
So don't get misled by this kid's pretty mug.

The puck's in the net—at least somewhere near it?
It still wouldn't count. He's got no school spirit.

REFEREE:
The puck's in the net, and when that's where it lands,
The only call possible's "Johnny's goal stands."

HOCKEY MOM:
That Johnny just got here. He came last September.
His mother is foreign, and she's not a member
Of one of our churches. So what's to discuss?
I've just said he's foreign. He's not one of us.

REFEREE:
Go sit down, lady.

To say Barack was someone to be feared
They used the robo-caller who had smeared
McCain himself—and just eight years before,
When Rove and Dubya launched their dirty war.
Back then, McCain, when he was asked his views,
Called that a tactic he would never use.
So now, the gasbags pondered, on and on,
Was that McCain of yore completely gone?
Not quite. It still was possible to gain
Some glimpses of that other John McCain—
Rebuking crowds when hateful words were spewed

(For doing that, McCain himself was booed)
And ordering his minions not to cite
The name and words of Jeremiah Wright.
In cautioning one vitriolic fan,
He called Barack "a good and decent man."
But signs of magnanimity were rare.
With Sarah Palin, they were just not there.
Her rallies fed red meat without remission.
Their underpinning was a definition:
Americans are small-town folks and such.
The people in big cities? Not so much.
This simplifies the issues quite a lot:
Some folks are real Americans, some not.
So it was easy for this hockey mother
To treat Barack Obama as the Other.
At hateful shouts, she only smiled and winked.
With her, the wink and snarkiness are linked.

"He's Not One of Us"

As John McCain's chances seem weakened or dead,
Republican rallies become mobs instead.
They have no civility left—not a shred.
They curse at Obama, their faces bright red.
"A traitor!" "A terrorist!" "Off with his head!"
"He's not one of us," Sarah Palin had said.
Lucky him.

The final candidate debate now loomed.
Some said that John McCain's campaign was doomed
Unless in this debate he changed the game.
He said, his gloves now off, that was his aim.
He couldn't shake Barack, though, from his mooring,
And most of all this last debate was boring.
The winner, polls concluded, was the guy
Who only needed something like a tie.
McCain did fine; the game, though, was unchanged.
The status quo had not been rearranged.
The only change politicos could gauge
Was this: One Joe the Plumber came on stage.
McCain said Joe would take a mighty blow
On taxes if Obama ran the show.
It turned out Joe would not be in that bracket.
It turned out, once the press had caused its racket,
A lot of Joe was, to be kind, invented.
But John McCain maintained Joe represented
The spreading of the wealth Obama sought.
Joe symbolized instead, some others thought,
That John McCain's campaign staff wasn't getting
A whole lot better when it came to vetting.

29

The Finish

Endorsements for Obama started swelling.
The ones that were particularly telling
Were from Republicans. They formed a shield
Against the charge he came from far left field.
(It always had been difficult to deem
So calm a person dangerously extreme.)
Then William Buckley's son, and Reagan's too,
Said John McCain and Palin wouldn't do.
(By then, Barack's donation list had duly
Recorded dough from Nixon's daughter Julie.
Would all Right-diaper babies now jump ship?
Would John Podhoretz and Bill Kristol flip?
Would Democrats get funded by some lady
Who boasted Herbert Hoover as her *zayde*?)
Then Colin Powell offered voters surety
That cred was there on national security:

The most respected soldier in the land
Had said Barack was ready to command.

The Republicans Change to a New Robo-Call Message After Colin Powell Endorses Barack Obama on Meet the Press

Well, Powell is Obama's friend.
He said so on the show.
And this Obama worked with Ayers.
We thought you'd want to know.

Yes, Powell pals around with pals
Of terrorists. It's proved.
If he's no terrorist himself.
He's simply once removed.

Some papers that you'd think you couldn't force
With heinous torture ever to endorse
A Democratic candidate now wrote
That Senator Obama had their vote.
Most writers of these pieces made the case
That picking Palin, though it pleased the base,
Was irresponsible and had reversed
The notion that McCain put Country First.

(The voting public basically agreed,
For this is what the polls showed they believed:
To hold the post to which she now aspired
Some qualities she lacked would be required.)
This pick, the papers wrote, did not suggest
Decision-making at its very best.
By then, it seemed McCain might lose the game,
So jockeying began for whom to blame.
Who'd be the scapegoat in the final score?
It seemed that Palin might be picked once more.

Sarah Palin's Bubble Deflates Just as Her Clothing Bills Arrive

At first it seemed daring—a bold McCain stroke.
His choice of Ms. Palin proved he'd go for broke.
Conservatives loved her. She held them in thrall.
They thought, "This McCain's not so bad after all."
Because of that start it's now hard to believe a
McCain camp lieutenant would call her a diva.
Well, politics sure isn't beanbag or cricket,
And now there's no doubt she's a drag on the ticket.
They dressed her all up. They could put her in Prada,
But what she can say that's of substance is nada.
Folks say it was reckless, considering oldness,
For John to pick Sarah. Well, so much for boldness.

October passed without the big surprise,
And Democrats began to realize
What caused this dread they'd felt from the beginning:
They were, no doubt, in danger now of winning.
The polling looked consistently auspicious;
It looked too good. That made them superstitious.
They carried charms and made weird signs to try
To stave off mischief from the Evil Eye.
The pundits turned this period yet more frightening
With knowing chats on how the race was tightening.
More nervousness was there election night.
Obamacans, in clutches, all sat tight
To see if networks truly would project
Obama as the president-elect.
The fear that the election might be stolen
Could give a Democrat a spastic colon.
Despite its technoprops, TV seemed slow
In telling voters what they had to know.
And then, almost abruptly, they could say
Obama is to lead the U.S.A.
McCain, a man whom admirals begat,
Now did them proud. His gracious speech showed that,
However flawed the fall campaign he ran,
He is himself "a good and decent man."
Obama spoke to thousands in Grant Park
About the road on which we'd now embark.
And many thought, as he described that walk,
Yes, here's how presidents are meant to talk.
The TV showed the dancing and the cheers
And African Americans in tears.

And foreigners, from Rome to Yokohama,
Were cheering an American: Obama.
From this vote they were willing to infer
We aren't the people they had thought we were.
And Lady Liberty, as people call her,
Was standing in the harbor somewhat taller.

Race in America, November 5, 2008

The curse is not broken, as some would deduce.
The curse is so strong we may never break loose.
But now, at this moment, we cling to the theme
Set forth by the man who said, "I have a dream."